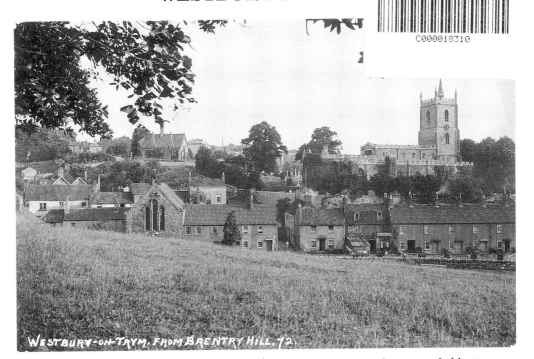

WESTBURY-ON-TRYM. FROM BRENTRY HILL. 72.

1. The village from Brentry Hill in about 1910. The parish church surrounded by trees. To the left the Wesleyan Church, and behind on the skyline the village hall.

The Village Hall, Westbury-on-Trym.

Sincock, The Library, Westbury-on-Trym.

2. The village hall built in 1869, situated at the top of Waters Lane in Eastfield Road. This postcard was postally used in 1908.

Institute & Fountain, Westbury -on- Trym.   Sincock. The Library, Westbury -on- Trym.

3. The centre of the village in c.1905, Stoke Lane left and the pointed roof of the men's club, erected as a memorial to F.W. and G.W. Savage in 1897, adjoining Canford Lane.

Westbury on Trym. 1168

4. Looking along Stoke Lane. The shop behind the fountain was owned by Frederick Sincock, who published many early postcards of Westbury.

5. Children gathered around the fountain built to commemorate Queen Victoria's Diamond Jubilee. The bus is about to depart for New Passage, connecting with the trams at the terminus in Westbury. This view c.1914.

6. The fountain from Westbury Hill c.1905, with Westbury Court Farm behind the trees.

Westbury Hill.

Harvey Barton's Series.

7. Westbury Hill in c.1902, before the trams came in 1908. The Methodist Church spire, just visible, was built in 1887.

Westbury Hill. No. 2.

Sincock. The Library, Westbury-on-Trym.

8. Further down Westbury Hill in c.1905, showing the many shops. The first owned by Taylor and Roach, Drapers & Milliners, with Westbury Subscription Library next door. The trees in the distance bordering Westbury Court Farm.

9. The tram terminus, with the War Memorial, erected in 1920, to the memory of the men who died fighting in the 1914-18 war. The fountain which stood on that position was re-erected in Canford Park.

10. The War Memorial looking towards High Street, in the 1930s. Trams No.6 and 4, awaiting their return journey to the Tramway centre. They continued in service until 1938, when buses were introduced on that route.

11. From the bottom of Westbury Hill looking towards Canford Lane, the Carlton Cinema can be seen just beyond the rank of shops. The cinema opened in 1933, and closed in 1959.

12. The Carlton Cinema in Canford Lane in the 1930s. The cottage in the middle distance adjoining Canford Park, and on the corner with Falcondale Road, served teas and ice cream until it was demolished in 1960.

WESTBURY ON TRYM

13. The High Street before 1914, a horse and cart, with its driver standing, wending his way home in the evening sun. The building by the lamp is Westbury on Trym Police Station built in 1869, beyond a sign on the wall Mealing Bros. engineering machinist and cycle works, and further along the Shoeing forge of P.J. Grigg & Son, Farriers.

14. The shop with the sun blinds down is on the corner of Henbury Road and Passage Road, on the opposite corner the White Lion Inn and Trym Road. The river Trym flows alongside this road, and then under the road at this point.

WESTBURY ON TRYM

Loe Christmasse itt now comyth
Soe eate and drynke youre fille —
Butte iffe ye toothsomme Turkeye
Shoulde happe toe make ye ille
Forgette not Hym who myselfhe
Ye cumminge Dose and pills
Alle for hys friende ye Fedder man
Who dwelleth att ye mille

(old English Ballad)

With best wishes for the festive Season

May good digestion wait upon appetite — also (health)

arcadia (?)

15. The oldest part of Westbury, looking at Dail House from the bottom of Chock Lane. This Christmas Greeting card written in old English was posted in 1902.

DIAL HOUSE, WESTBURY-ON-TRYM. 9249.

16. Dail House from Trym Road in 1936, the turning left is Channells Hill.

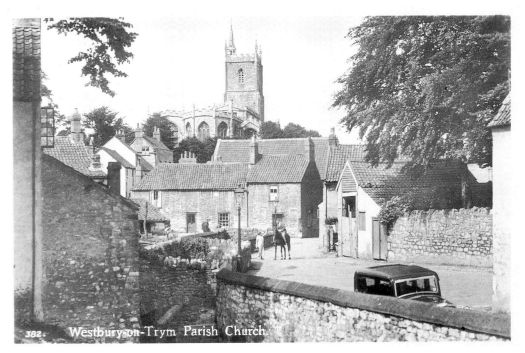

17. Another 1930s view of the old village, with the Parish Church high on the hill behind, the cottages in the middle of the picture are at the bottom of Chock Lane, now replaced by flats called Trym House.

18. The College was built 1459-69 as a residence for the Deans and Canons of Westbury Church. Burnt down by Prince Rupert in 1643, to prevent occupation by the Parliamentary Forces, only the Gatehouse remains. The property was purchased in 1894, and invested in the National Trust in 1907. This view c.1910.

19. Stoke Lane looking towards the centre of Westbury in 1926. Houses built at the turn of the century are mixed with properties built in the 1920s. The open topped car parked is Reg. No. H T 6995.

20. Stoke Lane, one of the longest roads in Westbury, extends from Parrys Lane and wends its way across Falcondale Road to the village. This view of Stoke Lane shows the two Inns, the Black Swan and further along the Prince of Wales.

21. Henbury Hill, a carriage descending towards Westbury in 1913. The tower of the church is visible with the pointed roof of the village hall adjoining. The fields beyond the wall are now all developed with housing.

22. Stoke Park with its large, mostly detached houses in Stoke Lane, extending along from the corner with Charlcombe Road. The only difference today from this c.1906 view, is the first house on the right which has been replaced by modern shops and flats.

23. Falcondale Road with the woods of Blaise Castle Estate beyond, in the late 1920s early 1930s. Westbury on Trym Library is further along on the left, at the corner with Canford Lane.

24. Abbey Road connects with Stoke Lane, and on the left hand side the houses back onto sports grounds, and further along Canford Park, emerging in Falcondale road.

25. Canford Lane from the entrance to Canford Cemetery when still a narrow road. The sculptors and masons shop owned by Cox Bros, was in business there in c.1932.

26. Canford Cemetery with the chapel of rest, and its distinctive pointed roof, in the early 1930s.

27. Canford Park with small children sitting on a seat in front of the bandstand, with the park keeper standing by. This early 1920s view is looking in the direction of Canford Lane.

28. Canford Park showing the walled formal garden, with a large fish pond, in the 1930s.

29. Falcondale Road built as a Bypass for the village of Westbury. This view, in the direction of Westbury Road, shows houses newly built and open spaces awaiting development.

30. The top of the hill leading into the village, in Westbury Road. The junction on the right leading to Eastfield Road.

Westbury Road. No. 3.
Do you recognise this lodge.

Sincock, Henleaze

31. Westbury Road in 1906, the turning for Henleaze Gardens beyond the two horse and carts. In the centre distance the Lodge to Badminton House.

Badminton House, Junior School, Westbury-on-Trym.

32. Badminton House School situated in spacious grounds off of Westbury Road, This view is of the original house, approached from the lodge entrance, by a drive. Still a flourishing school today with many extensions and buildings around the original house.

WESTBURY ROAD.

33. Westbury Road from the corner with Brecon Road, a tram approaching. On the right the wall and trees surrounding the grounds of Badminton School.

Westbury Road. No. 4   Sincock,

34. In the opposite direction, workmen by the wall of Badminton House grounds. No tram lines can be seen in the picture so it must have been taken before 1908.

The Red Maids' School, Westbury-on-Trym, Bristol. The School.

35. The Red Maids School, with its spacious grounds in Westbury Road. This view shows the original house, Burfield. The school moved to Westbury in 1911 from the original building in Denmark Street, near the city centre.

The Red Maids' School, Westbury-on-Trym, Bristol. A View of the Grounds.

36. Red Maid girls in the gardens in front of the house. Red Maids School was founded by Alderman Whitson in 1627. He bequeathed in his will certain property to provide forty poor girls with education.

37. During the 1914-18 War the school house was used as a war hospital. Recuperating soldiers are standing in the main porch, with patriotic flags flying from the roof.

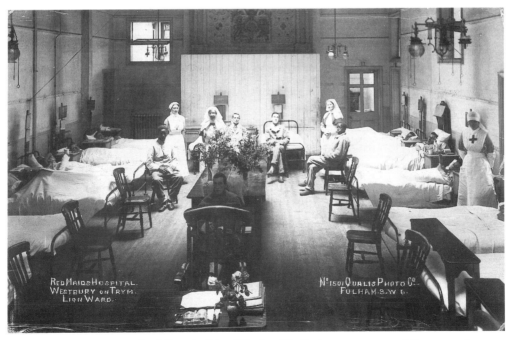

38. An interior view of soldiers in Lion Ward, with their nurses, one of the many large rooms taken over as a hospital ward in the school.

The Red Maids' School. Westbury-on-Trym, Bristol. The Library.

39. Girls studying in the school Library c.1914. The founder decreed in his will that the girls wear red dresses, with white ribbons, and tippets, and for outdoor wear straw hats trimmed with blue, and red cloaks.

40. A 1930s view of Red Maids School showing most of the buildings which make up the school and the extensive grounds at that time.

41. Henleaze Road from the corner with Henleaze Avenue, further along the road are shops, which are still a busy shopping area today. Postcard published locally by C.H. Morrish and posted in November 1906.

42. In the same road showing the lower rank of shops between Cavendish Road and Cardigan Road. Postcard published by F.C. Sincock of Henleaze c.1908.

43. The view of the shops towards Cavendish Road in 1918. The shop by the postbox owned by F.C. Sincock, publisher of many local postcards.

44. Henleaze Road in the opposite direction in June 1935. Traffic now in evidence, but the extreme right corner yet to be removed for road widening.

45. Henleaze Gardens from Westbury Road. The postcard was published by C.H. Morrish of Henleaze, and postally used in November 1909.

46. Henleaze Gardens in the opposite direction from Henleaze Road. This postcard was postally used in December 1919.

47. Henleaze Avenue which connects Henleaze Road with Westbury Road. The postcard was posted in May 1922, but probably published a few years earlier.

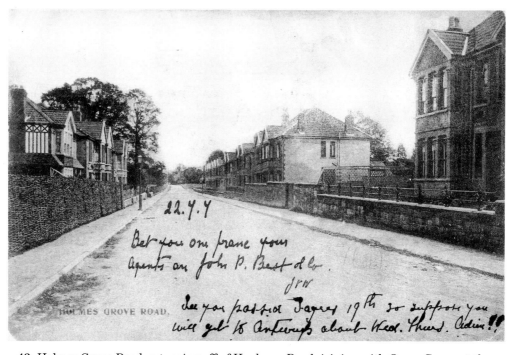

48. Holmes Grove Road, a turning off of Henleaze Road, joining with Owen Grove at the far end. This postcard postally used in July 1907.

49. Cavendish Road in c.1930, this postcard was published locally by F.C. Sincock.

50. This postcard was written and posted from 16 Cavendish Road in June 1911, showing the interesting detail of the double bay semi-detached houses built at the turn of the century, in this part of Henleaze.

51. Dublin Crescent joining Henleaze Road by the present day post office, and merging with Waterford Road. This view looks towards the far end connecting with Brecon Road in c.1930.

52. An aerial view of Henleaze Park in 1928. Henleaze Park House became St. Margarets School in 1915, and to the right can be seen Claremont House. Many of the roads in the foreground were not fully developed.

53. Henleaze Lane known today as Henleaze Road. The present day post office is situated by the second horse and cart, and opposite Henley Grove Lodge, the lodge to Henley Park House. The former house was situated between the present Lawrence and Owen Groves. This picture c.1905.

54. Henleaze Congregational Church built in 1907. This view in Henleaze Road looking in the direction of the shops, the church known today as Henleaze United Reform Church. This view is from 1909, before road widening, in later years.

55. The Thatched Lodge. One of the entrances to Henleaze Park Estate is the drive on the right, and a very narrow Henleaze Road. The Lodge survives today. Postcard published by F.C. Sincock and posted in October 1906.

56. Grange Park, a long road of mainly detached houses. It extends from Waterford Road in Henleaze to Priory Avenue and Eastfield Terrace in Westbury On Trym.

The Convent, Henleaze.

57. The Sisters of Mercy bought the Convent in 1896, for a boarding school, named St. Ursulas, and it is still a school today. This view c.1905 before Brecon Road was developed.

Marjorie's School.   St. Ursula's High School. Playing Field.

58. St. Ursulas High School playing fields bordering Brecon Road showing the extensive convent buildings surrounded by trees. The postcard was sent from No.3 Brecon Road in January 1931.

59. Henleaze Road looking towards Westbury and Southmead in the 1920s. Beyond the cottages the original Eastfield Inn. The present day Eastfield Inn was built on the site in the 1930s, and the cottages demolished in 1964 for the building of a petrol station.

60. The two cottages with trellis work porches and the trees beyond bordering the Blind School were removed for road widening in the early 1920s. Express Dairies (formerly Ropers Dairy) now operate opposite the terraced cottages.

61. The Quarry, approached from Lake Road, from the junction with Eastfield Road and Southmead Road. This picture was taken not long after quarrying was discontinued in c.1912. The remains of the Quarry buildings are on the right.

62. The Quarry became known as Henleaze Lake. It became a popular pool for swimming, a club was formed in 1919 and is still popular today. This view shows the extensive stretch of water towards Badock Woods.

63. The Blind School entrance from Southmead Road before 1914. The earlier Blind School was in Queens Road near the top of Park Street. Bristol University was built on the site, opening in c.1925.

64. The Blind School from the drive, showing the extensive front of the school with its distinctive clock and bell tower in c.1912. The school was demolished in 1971 in favour of modern housing.

65. The Beehive Inn in Wellington Hill West. This view is of the original Inn in 1935, the proprietor Mr. E. Hunt. In the late 1930s the new Beehive Inn was built at the time advertising large ornamental grounds and gardens, and skittle alley, with parking for seventy cars.

66. Southmead Road looking in the direction of Henleaze. The post office and supply stores proprietor E. Banfield, established in 1885. A delightful family group outside their terraced cottage in 1915.

67. Westbury Road from the White Tree, with a distant view of St. Monicas Home behind the trees.

68. St. Monicas Home was built on the site of Cote House which was sold in 1918. It was demolished and replaced by St. Monicas in c.1925. Mr. H.H. Wills named it after his wife.

69. Durdham Downs from North View, the large houses facing the Downs is Westbury Park. This postcard was postally used in 1913.

WESTBURY PARK, DURDHAM DOWN.

70. Westbury Park, the tree lined road looking in the opposite direction towards the White Tree.

71. North View from the Downs, a Tram travelling along Westbury Road towards Westbury On Trym. Looking into North View, a bank on the corner of Downs Park West, c.1914.

72. North View in the early 1930s. Note the early Petrol Pump in Durdham Down Garage. The shops and terraced cottages are much the same today.

73. North View c.1913. The terraced houses beyond the shops, with Devonshire Road the turning by the letter box. In the distance are the back gardens of the houses in Howard Road.

74. Downs Park West in c.1918. A few undeveloped sites amongst the large houses already built. The road joins with Henleaze Road from North View.

75. Berkeley Road Westbury Park, connecting with Etloe Road and joining Devonshire Road at the other end. Four small children standing outside the shop. The postcard postally used in October 1912.

76. Victoria Road, a cul de sac off of Etloe Road. The stationery and general store was owned by Mr. M. Pidgeon. Note the row of different size dustbins! This view is on a postally used postcard in 1916.

77. Etloe Road looking towards the White Tree on Durdham Downs. The shop on the left is a hardware store advertising Pullars Dye Works, Perth, Scotland. Opposite an advertisement for tea noted blend 1/6d (7½p) and special blend 1/8 (8p)! Postcard published by Mr. M. Pidgeon of Victoria Road Westbury Park, whose shop is shown in illustration 76.

78. Westbury Park Primary School, built in c.1895, and when first built called a Board School. The school is situated near the beginning of Bayswater Avenue. The postcard postally was used in January 1908.

St. Alban's Church, Westbury Park.

79. St. Albans Church on the corner of Bayswater Avenue and Coldharbour Road. This is a very early view of the first church, note the rough road. The postcard was posted in 1908.

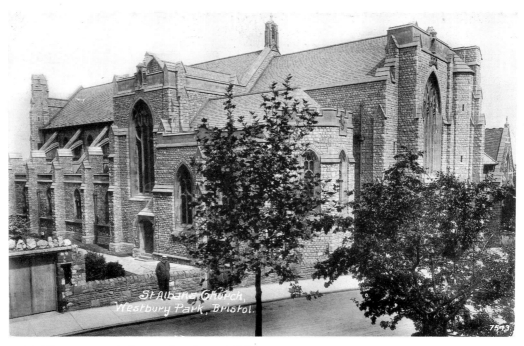

St Albans Church, Westbury Park, Bristol.

80. The new, much larger church, in Coldharbour Road. The pointed roof of the earlier church just visible on the right.

81. Devonshire Road in c.1913. It joins North View at the other end of Coldharbour Road. The neat double bay villas were built at the turn of the century.

82. St. Albans Road runs parallel with Devonshire Road, connecting with the same two roads. The trees in both roads survive today, some newly planted.

83. Coldharbour Road c.1907. Devonshire Road is the turning on the left, looking towards the shops, another postcard published locally by M. Pidgeon of Westbury Park.

84. Coldharbour Road at the junction with Linden Road. The caption on the card reads Redland, it is on the border with Westbury Park. This view, c.1922, shows the terraced houses of Halsbury Road in the middle distance.

85. Howard Road, a turning from Linden Road, and connecting with Springfield Grove at the other end, part of the road awaiting development in c.1912.

86. Linden Road in Redland on the edge of Westbury Park. This is a 1930s view with Howard Road the turning on the left, and by the cyclist St. Albans Road.

INDEX

A
Abbey Road 24

B
Badminton House 32
Beehive Public House 65
Berkeley Road 75
Blind School 63, 64

C
Cavendish Road 49, 50
College 18
Canford Lane 12, 25
Canford Park 27, 28
Congregational Church 54
Convent 59
Coldharbour Road 83, 84

D
Dail House 15, 16
Devonshire Road 81
Dublin Crescent 51
Durham Down 69
Downs Park West 74

E
Etloe Road 77

F
Falcondale Road 23, 29

G
Grange Park 56

H
High Street 5, 6, 11, 13, 14
Henbury Hill 21
Henleaze Avenue 47
Henleaze Road 41, 42, 43, 44, 59, 60
Henleaze Gardens 45, 46
Henleaze Park 52
Henleaze Lane 53
Henleaze Lake 61, 62
Henleaze Park Lodge 55
Holmes Grove Road 48
Howard Road 85

L
Linden Road 86

N
North View 71, 72, 73

P
Parish Church 17

R
Red Maids School 35, 36, 37, 38, 39, 40

S
Stoke Lane 19, 20
Stoke Park 22
Southmead Road 66
St. Monica's Home 68
St. Ursula's School 58
St. Albans Church 79, 80
St. Albans Road 82
School 78

V
View of Westbury 1
Victoria Road 76

W
Westbury Hill 7, 8
Westbury Park 70
Westbury Road 30, 31, 33, 34, 67
Westbury Village 3, 4, 21
Westbury Village Hall 2
War Memorial 9, 10